PROFOUNDLY

RELEVANT MEDITATIONS

PROFOUNDLY RELEVANT
MEDITATIONS

written by matt collura

cover photograph by james chororos

Charleston, SC
www.PalmettoPublishing.com

Profoundly Relevant Meditations

ISBN - 13: 978-1-64990-288-7
ISBN - 10: 1-64990-288-3

dedicated to my mom, my dad,

and Alicia

BEAUTY AND THE BEAST

COUSINS

SISTER & BROTHER

HALLOWS

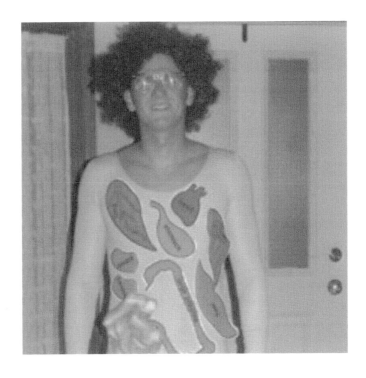

Contents

What does it all mean?!

yay! - inspirational posts

yes! - conclusive posts about life, humanity,and
the self

yes!? - open-ended posts about life, humanity,
and the self

yeah... - miscellaneous

foreword

On March 9, 2011, Matt Collura suffered a traumatic brain injury in a snowboarding accident.

In addition, Matt suffered several broken ribs, two collapsed and punctured lungs, a broken wrist, and broken fingers. For weeks he laid in his ICU bed in a coma, unresponsive to outside stimuli and unable to regulate even the most basic functions without the aid of wires, tubes, machines, and a team of doctors and nurses.

There was a steady stream of visitors to his room including family, friends, teachers, and coaches. There was a notebook at his bedside, and visitors were encouraged to write about their relationship with Matt. The stories and comments were replete with accounts of how Matt encouraged, helped, and comforted them in their most troubled times, how he made them laugh when they were down, and how he inspired them to tackle difficult tasks when they were unsure of themselves.

In high school, Matt was captain of three sports teams. He graduated with a degree in biochemistry from Boston College and a master's in architecture from NJIT. These accomplishments pale in comparison when measured against the joy, happiness, and inspiration he brings to many of those who know him.

As he gradually awoke from his coma and began a long, challenging road to recovery, his friends and family said "If anyone can make it through this, it's Matt."

And they were right. Over the past nine years, the same dedication that drove his athletic and academic successes has driven his remarkable recovery. Far surpassing many doctors' predictions, Matt is able to walk with a walker, speak very clearly (if not perfectly), and continues to work tirelessly to improve and eventually live independently.

Before his accident, Matt started a blog on a whim and ironically called it *Profoundly Relevant Meditations*. Most of the entries were funny, ridiculous, or just plain weird. However, after his accident and before he was able to speak, he communicated with a keyboard on his iPad. Eventually he started to chronicle his recovery through his blog by making daily entries including his deepest thoughts on life's challenges from his unique perspective. Some entries are inspirational, some contain philosophical insights, some are just silly, but all are entertaining.

Matt selected his favorite posts for this book. They contain thoughts and ideas that will move you to tears and laughter. Hopefully you will be inspired to face your life challenges, as Matt has, with humor, wisdom, strength, and dignity, and in spite of all of the odds, rise above them.

Mom and Dad

about the author

My name is Matt. I am the progenitor of this book and the blog of the same name. I suffered a traumatic brain injury in a snowboarding accident on March 9, 2011. That event drastically changed my life. Recovering from my brain injury empowers me with rare wisdom. I often share this wisdom on my blog, and thus reading it and this book is worthwhile. Also, some of my entries are pretty funny.

about the blog

Profoundly Relevant Meditations is a blog I created in 2007. It contains inspirational, insightful, and comedic entries. I do not focus it toward a specific population of people. That, to me, is the beauty of it. I cater my entries to no specific group, but to any member of the human species. So if you are anybody, my blog is for you.

introduction

present to you a collection of my finest blog entries. If you like my blog, you will like this book. If you have never read my blog: I mean, come on. You must not understand its magnificence, are ignorant to its grandeur, or you have just never heard of it. Visit www.profoundlyrelevantmeditations.com now (or immediately after you read this book)!   I have organized this book in chapters according to a consistent theme. The posts are in reverse chronological order.

yay!

1

2020.06.12

you are strong

We sometimes feel unable to live.
Everyone, at times,
thinks he or she cannot continue.
We all sink into a mindset
controlled by malaise.
This mindset, if you keep it weak,
is only temporary.
Our will is always there:
strong and ready to be used.
You are strong.
Your inner strength,
although it seems
nonexistent at times,
is there. Just remember to
find your strength,
and be strong.

soul's world

I still have times when sadness compounds.
I still think "Why must I live like this?"
and "Where can I find joy?"
Yet, I am generally happy.
My happiness does not come from
making an excellent physical recovery.
I do not look to running to find joy.
Running is years, if not lifetimes, away.
Rather, happiness comes
from a positive mindset.
Gone are the days when I
desperately chase a dream dependent on
my brain's tenuous connection to my body.
I now have a stronger dependence on
my brain's accessible
connection to my soul.
Where my brain-body
connection finds little joy,
the available brain-soul
connection compensates.
My body lives in a world limited by disability.
However, my soul lives in a world
without limits.

capitalize on circumstance.

The extra layer
to the saying,
"It's all about
being in the right place,
at the right time."
is "It's all about making
the right decision,
in the right place,
at the right time."
Sure, circumstance guide life,
to a certain degree.
It does no good
to make the wrong decision
in the right place,
at the right time.
Yes, luck is a factor in life.
But it does not control life.
We control life by
not letting luck control us.

2020.06.08

inevitable

Do you know how it feels
to be so passionate about
achieving something,
that the thought of failure
never enters your mind?
You know you will not fail,
because you will not give up.
You will try until you succeed.

2020.05.31

succeed

Experiences teach us. Words do not.
We learn by trying, not by listening.
You must escape doubt and do it.
You may not succeed the first time.
But through trying, you will be more apt
to succeed the next time around.
Do not let the thought of failure
deter you from succeeding.

2020.03.19

life keeps going, and so do you.

Life does not quit.
So you mustn't.

compete

There are levels to competition. On one level, we compete against others. On another level, we compete against ourself, or our impulse to quit. I am more concerned with the latter level, as we must live with ourself. Every second we fight; sometimes more than others. But it is a constant battle. Are you winning the fight?

2019.11.02

you are able

Self-doubt, not lack of potential, is the main contributor to inability.

living my life (making you smile)

The news that I
suffered a traumatic brain injury
may have upset you.
The fact that I fight to do
nearly everything
may make you think,
"How can he live like that?"
That I can no longer run
may make you pity me.
I want to tell you:
do not be upset; do not pity me.
My life is better now than it ever has been.
I went from confused and insecure
to confident and insightful.
That makes me smile.
And it should make you smile too.

2019.03.23

find your strength.

Do not let physical weakness limit you.
Exterior inability does not mean
interior disability.
Many never take the time
to see the strength inside.
A frail beggar could be
a king or queen inside.
He or she maybe never
took the time to look.
You may find strength if you search.

battling

Every moment is a battle.
Something inside us pulls us
toward the path of least resistance.
This thing is strong, but we are stronger.
We beat this thing to the ground.
Resilient, we stand and think,
"I have what it takes to win."
We continue to fight. Day after day,
we wake up and fight
to accomplish many things.
It is okay, because we are strong.
We are never exalted for living.
We do not make headlines
for beating ourselves.
We can do this. We are happy to do this.
We are happy to be here.
We are happy to live.

2019.01.16

forever strong

You may think,
    "I am a slave to an unpredictable existence."
Things may threaten your livelihood
and compromise you physically.
In reality, nothing ever weakens you.
Meet exterior forces with unwavering strength.
That which impedes you physically
is a chance to showcase your inner fortitude.
You have undying strength.
You are in control of your resilience and dignity.

2018.12.12

happy nightmare

Being in a wheelchair was my worst nightmare.
I had an accident.
Now, I am living my one-time nightmare.
Back when I was training for a marathon,
I never imagined my nightmare would
test my strength like nothing can,
make me a better man,
bring amazing people into my life,
and result in heightened self-esteem.
I now realize I am not living my nightmare.
My nightmare is turning into someone
whose world is dark and disabled,
not someone in a wheelchair.
My world is far from dark or disabled.
In a wheelchair I can find happiness
greater than I ever imagined.

2018.12.11

control

Do not give the uncontrollable environment control over your outlook.
External things change on a whim.
Allow your mind to control your outlook.
The environment is strong.
But the human mind is stronger.
The beauty of being human is
standing up to negative change
with unwavering positivity.

challenges

Challenges appear anywhere.
They are unavoidable.
Even if you desire to live lazily,
it is a challenge to sustain a lazy lifestyle.
If you want to run a marathon,
it is a challenge to run 26.2 consecutive miles
without giving up or passing out.
No matter what, we all face challenges.
To a large extent,
your ability to welcome challenges
represents your willingness to live.

2018.11.10

problems?

U se of the word "problems" is problematic. We only call prob-lems "problems" because we identify them as such. Why should I see my wheelchair use as a "problem" instead of an opportunity to empower myself and inspire others? My life is not full of problems but opportunities.

2018.10.10

value of things

see little value in labeling things as favorable or unfavorable. Whether good or bad, we gain something from everything. The "good" things give us a reason to continue while the "bad" things give us character.

2018.08.04

a better time

I sometimes want to go back
to time a time when I could run,
when children did not ask,
"What is wrong with him?"
and when I was listened to.
If I could go back to my past life: I would run,
people would understand my words,
and I would be "normal."
But I would not be secure,
know my own strength,
understand tragedy,
have invaluable perspective,
and realize the trauma I can rehabilitate from.
When I think about it,
I wonder why I would go back.
I would not accept myself, not be happy,
and not know now is a better time.

2018.07.26

continue

When you try, you may fail.
But you can also succeed.
If you try, do not focus on your failures.
Focus on your successes.
Continue trying, and continue succeeding.

2018.07.07

test yourself.

Test your limits.
Do not think you cannot improve.
Believe me: you can improve.
You will be pleased when you make the
improbable possible.

2018.05.12

something

Animals making miraculous recoveries from debilitating physical injuries is amazing. Animals have no high-level understanding of the benefits of recovering physically. They just do it. And they do not complain. Watching a viral video of a dachshund rehabilitate from a spinal cord injury inspires me. A certain unidentified type of will drives us all to improve.

2018.05.06

game time!

I want my old brain back. And I want to run a marathon. Both of those things would be fantastic. If I had my pre-2011 brain and I could run a marathon, it would be game time! All of my dreams would be fulfilled. But wait: neither of those things are realistic. And in order for me to be happy, I must face reality. What is realistic? I survived severe head trauma. I could be dead. But I am alive. And I live a challenged life. Maybe game time for me is welcoming challenges. Realizing this, I say, "Bring on the challenges, life. It's game time!"

2018.02.19

trying

People tell me I will never run again. I do not concern myself with that. I am at peace with parting ways with running. I may not run again, but that does not mean I will give up. I may die before I start running, but I will die before I stop trying.

I make many mistakes,
and I beat myself up over them.
I often think,
"I know too much to be that stupid."
But if I did not make any mistakes,
I would have no wisdom.
I should not focus on my mistakes
but on the lessons learned.

only you

Nobody other than you can define the limits of your ability. While I lay in a coma, doctors said I would never sit up straight again. Doctors may know medicine, but they do not know me. Med school cannot convey the immeasurable strength of the human spirit. Test the limits of your ability. Do not allow others to define your limits. Only you know your limits.

2017.06.30

running is a state of mind.

My definition of running differs from the dictionary's definition. For me, running is not about balance, speed, distance, or relative ability. Rather, running is about living on the limits of your own ability. Reaching these limits provokes a feeling of euphoria commonly called "runner's high." I do not physically run, but through hard work, I achieve a runner's euphoric state of mind. This state of mind makes me feel like I once felt, like a "runner."

spirit

Sure, they have odds for a man to battle back from a traumatic injury. But those odds are just an average. There are outliers in an average. With exceptional spirit, one can become an outlier. It is all about the human spirit.

yes!

photograph by James Chororos

2020.10.03

accept imperfection.

L ife is mainly a process of acceptance.
Life is not perfect, nor will it ever be perfect.
Almost nothing, save circles, is perfect.
Accept imperfection, and do the best with what you have.
It is not about striving for perfection.
It is about making the best out of imperfection.

2020.09.16

spread that goodness!

I like being around good people. Good people enhance my positive traits and make me better, to the extent that I can then influence them with my own goodness. Goodness spreads. The positive energy I emit to the good people around me will subsequently spread outside of my circle of goodness. In this way, my positivity grows exponentially, endlessly. I make the world a better place by spreading goodness.

2020.09.03

kill yourself (with kindness)

I am easily aggravated. Basically anyone can frustrate me; even if I love you (ESPECIALLY if I love you (ask my mom and dad)). One thing I have been doing lately is killing MYSELF with kindness. When someone, who I otherwise like, begins to bug me, I replace the negative thoughts of him or her with positive ones. I will then be intentionally kind to that person to enhance my positive thinking. This approach increases the positivity I feel toward people and promotes overall good mental health.

2020.08.20

perspective

Someone always has it worse. Sometimes when my disability has me feeling bad for myself, I think of persons who were born with a permanent disability. I, at least, can gain abilities back through hard work and discipline. I then stop moping and start working.

2020.07.30

avoid drowning in lemonade.

Sometimes it is more about taking lemons and not making lemon juice than it is about taking lemons and making lemonade. Bad things with no potential to be turned into lemonade just happen. We cannot always add sugar to a bad situation to create a great taste. We sometimes need to accept badness as bad, not squeeze out a sour taste, and come out better on the other side. Sugarcoating life, as if you can put a positive spin on everything, is living a lie. Living in a fantasy world will make you seem insane and ultimately make you bitter. Live in reality, accept that bad things happen, sustain any badness, and enjoy the goodness that awaits.

2020.07.27

learn to adapt

Things are always changing.
Sometimes, the thing you hope
would stay the same changes.
I hoped to run my whole life.
One day, running was taken away.
Do I still think about running? Yes.
Do I cry? Yes. Do I sulk? No.
Do I maximize what I have? Yes.
Things do not always stay constant.
One thing that must stay constant
is knowing how to adapt
and doing the best with what you have.

2020.07.26

"problem" solving

Sometimes, solving a problem is about realizing that what you see as a "problem" is not really a problem.

2020.07.17

be different.

Being different is hard. The desire for commonality often discourages us from following our individual preferences. If society never accepts any of your differences, be satisfied that you are who you want to be. The ideas of an individual are often clearer and more focused than collective ideas. Society often applauds phenomenon that later becomes commonly accepted as soulless garbage. Furthermore, some of your differences may one day be accepted by popular culture. In an area you were once shunned as an outcast, you have become a "pioneer." The happiness you receive from others praising your one-time differences, or just from being yourself, far outweighs any happiness you receive from fitting in. This happiness justifies being different.

2020.05.05

a reality of singularity

I am unique.
We are unique.
Sometimes, we lose our
unique characteristics
in an attempt to fit in.
Society focuses too much
on making us all the same:
one of the impossible aspirations of society.
Instead of trying to fulfill an invisible wish;
realize, fulfill, and take pleasure in
the reality that we are all unique.

2020.04.05

determined to be yourself

Thoughts come and go.
Emotions come and go.
We remain.
We are not our thoughts,
or our emotions.
We must face the capricious
tide of thoughts and emotions
with unwavering strength.
Do not let this
whimsical wave
deter you from your path.
Be who you want to be.

2019.04.30

you are living.

Do you ever stop to think, "It is such a blessing to just be alive?" And then you stop thinking about your life and start doing something with it…

worn

I want to become sea glass.
The ocean waves run over
manufactured jagged glass,
and return it to its smooth, natural state.
I am so coarse, so rough.
I have acquired so much.
I am the product of human involvement.
Throw me into the ocean.
Let the waves wash over me
and make me natural.

2018.08.27

healing

We cannot heal without effort. No matter the severity of the injury, we all need to expend energy to rehabilitate. For instance, a minor abrasion will not heal if you make no effort to protect it. You cannot just leave a cut exposed as if nothing happened.

My brain injury teaches me the severity of this phenomenon. For me to rehabilitate, I need to work on my musculature and my emotions regularly. I will not wake up one day, start running, and feel perfect. I need to do therapy daily to improve. We are all healing physically and emotionally. As much as we may not want to, we need to work to heal.

2018.08.26

act.

Some long to know before doing.
One cannot know before doing.
We learn through experience. After all,
we are not equipped with knowledge.
We are equipped with the
ability to acquire knowledge.
Act and learn how to succeed.

2018.07.08

repayment

The world will ultimately treat you nicely in return for being a good person. As much as you might feel like your positivity goes unnoticed, the goodwill you emit will one day come back to you. I cannot promise you this, because I am not omniscient. Nor am I wise enough to know. I just have faith in goodness.

2018.06.30

we make a vast impression.

People notice our actions.
We make a difference.
Each day we live, we make an impression.
The people who see us use us as an example.
Many people see us,
and many see those who see us.
In our life, we make many impressions.
If you realize your positive attributes
make an exponentially positive difference,
your days will add up to a happy lifetime.

2018.06.29

form your world.

You can focus on the things that bug you about life, or you can focus on the things that give you a reason to live. The things you focus on will ultimately form your image of reality. As much as you may think this is out of your control, the brain has an amazing ability to shape your world. Make the effort to form a positive reality.

2018.06.28

rational wheel

I do not believe the squeaky wheel gets the grease. If one is "squeaky," one may be labeled a complainer. The complaints coming from a complainer have low credibility and low likelihood of being fulfilled. I call "complaints" coming from a logical, rational person "concerns." "Concerns" have a better chance of getting the grease than a squeaky complaint. I believe the logical wheel gets the grease.

2018.06.18

We do not die.
With conception,
an eternal soul is born.
Our soul influences other souls
and introduces immortal ideas.
The soul is composed
of the beings we affect,
the things we construct,
and the ideas we create.
It gives life to the world.
When the body passes,
the eternal soul continues
to impact existence.

I learned lessons in
elementary school, high school,
college, graduate school,
and from my accident.
I learned lessons in life.
I have learned many lessons.
I now realize the most valuable lesson
was taught to me
by the ocean waves in my childhood.
If we were to pay attention, we may notice
important life lessons coming from
lifeless things.

yes!?

photograph by James Chororos

the seacrest analysis

I sometimes dream of
being rich and famous.
But I never dream of
being Ryan Seacrest.
Even with his wealth and fame,
his personality
makes his life unappealing.
I WOULD NOT want to be that guy.
I am happy being myself.
I will take my lack of fame,
my lack of wealth,
and my disability,
THANK YOU VERY MUCH.
I sometimes wonder,
"If I were Ryan Seacrest,
would I have any awareness
that I was once myself?"
Or would I just completely
inhabit Ryan Seacrest's mind,
without any idea
of the life I once had?
What would I be like:
an awful fame-seeker (like Seacrest)

or an all right guy (like myself — I think)?
This is an interesting investigation
into body snatching...

2019.11.17

i am sure of this...maybe.

Things occur chaotically,
in an organized way.
Everything happens
for a reason, randomly.
You can use logic
to tell what others are thinking,
no-one is a mind-reader,
and you cannot assume.
Women are very caring, sweet,
and manipulative.
Bros before hoes,
and there is a great woman
behind every great man.
History repeats itself,
and we are progressive.
And I am sure of at least one thing:
you cannot be sure of anything...
maybe.

existence...

We do not comprehend
the magnitudes of space and time.
We are either incomprehensibly large
or infinitesimally small.
Temporality, at its extremes,
is confounding.
A mackerel lays, on average,
500,000 eggs at a time.
Scientists estimate that
100 billion galaxies exist.
The average human spends
three years on the toilet in a lifetime.
Some nerve impulses travel at
390 feet per second.
When the specifics of
existence are considered,
reality is crazy.
Accept the insanity of life,
and be sane in an insane world.

2019.03.05

live in the real world (a world without condescension).

Condescension is primarily a result of us giving power to those who condescend. Someone who typically condescends talks down from a platform he or she creates. We give this imaginary platform power by letting the words affect us. Those who stand on a real platform built by hard work and/or ability generally do not feel the need to condescend. Typically, those who condescend do so in an imaginary world. If we stop giving credence to condescension, it may cease to exist.

void

One may fill the void with a lavish thing.
Another fills the void with a wedding ring.
Some will fill the void
with drugs to relieve.
Others fill the void
with goals to achieve.
I too have a void.
The source is not known.
It may come from fear of being alone.
Sometimes I wonder,
"Will this void persist?"
Other times I wonder,
"Does this void exist?"

yeah...

2020.10.23

oddly audible

So, I am at the grocery store the other day. Some guy in my aisle makes a loud fart sound, but there is no smell at all. This guy "farts" another time: again no smell. My curiosity at this no-smell phenomenon is unusually high. So thinking I might be too far for my olfactory senses to detect a scent, I move closer. He lets another one rip: still no smell. But I do notice the "fart" sound escaping his head.

I go, "What is going on man?! Your farts don't smell, and they seem to be coming from your head!"

He responds, "Oh, I'm just brain farting. I do it all the time. I've been having trouble keeping them silent lately."

final tickle

My friend always tells others, "I will tickle you to death."
Usually the other person and my friend just laugh and go on living. One day, my friend told another person, "I will tickle you to death."

The other person, not thinking much of it, said, "Oh yeah? I dare you."

So my friend tickled him, and he died.

2020.08.16

beneficial memory loss

One "benefit" of having issues with your short-term memory is that sometimes you forget ordering stuff for yourself online. And then, on the day it arrives, it feels like a cool surprise. You, in fact, ordered the item yourself. But, in fact, you were not expecting it.

name change (eventual buckling)

Fluffin (my capricious cat) requested her name be changed four different times from April 10th to May 22nd. These are the first three names she wanted:

1. Melissa Lancaster
2. Angela Bumbleberry
3. Petrie Bambleblouse

On May 22nd, in a moment of weakness, I legally changed her name to her fourth request. For familiarity's sake, we still call her "Fluffin." However, her name of record is now "Penelope Pinglepants." I wonder how long it will take her to come up with another ridiculous name…

2020.04.25

antisocial distancing

Because of Coronavirus, communal gatherings have become a thing of the past. I do not necessarily miss the social aspect of parties. I think I miss being antisocial at social gatherings.

rectal drops

I take eye drops to alleviate my chronic dry eye. It reads "for rectal application only" on the "eye drops" box I just received. I found this interesting. "Why do they want me to apply eye drops to my rectum?" I thought. So I did not drop them into my eye (or my rectum), and I brought the box to the nurse who works at my therapy. The nurse was flabbergasted.

"Eye drops?! That's a rectal ointment!" exclaimed the nurse.

"I do not even have an issue with my rectum! And why does it say 'Eye Drops' on the box?!" I replied emphatically.

"Fair point. That IS confusing. Must be a typo…I'll contact them about that," responded the nurse.

2019.07.04

good ol' smithy boy

Have you heard about that TV show Will Smith is working on? Yeah, he is playing the chief editor of a hip new newspaper located in Los Angeles. The show is called *The Fresh Prints of Bel-Air.*

chippen-village

Monroe Township (my hometown) has a senior living community called Monroe Village. Each individual unit has a living room, dining room, kitchen, bathroom, and bedroom: ideal for independent living. A common dining hall serves food for the residents, allowing a social dining experience. Monroe Village even has a Chippendales to provide entertainment for the senior women — rare and surprising, but true.

2018.06.12

dishes

I know a guy who is obsessed with clean dishes. He always admonishes me for using an incorrect dish-to-dishwasher loading procedure and then advises me on how to properly load. I make fun of him and say, "You think you are the dish police." Lately, I have been curious though. What if he actually is a dish police officer who works for the local dish police department? I should ask him.

juniper seeds

G uess what, reader?
Today is the first day of June!
Oh, how I adore this month.
I especially enjoy watching
the prairie dogs frolic in the meadow!
I remember the days
when Johnny and I would run
through Mr. Thompson's yard.
What a jovial man Mr. Thompson was!
I still taste his home cooking on my tongue!
I recall the times when Jones would carry me
through the fields as we sang melodies of old.
The days are fresh in mind when I would
swim with Lil Timmy in the Allegheny River
and fish for largemouth bass.
I yearn for the days when I would
sit with Edith by the brook,
as we chewed on Juniper seeds.
We chewed until the sun set,
until my father called from the hills.
One fateful day of chewing,
Edith mistakenly chewed
on an acorn poisoned with cyanide.

Poor Edith soon passed away.
And nobody, aside from me,
attended her funeral,
because Edith was
a reclusive pickpocket,
and her parents did not
care for her too much.

grandma's whip

You can barely see a face
buried behind those shades.
But she don't give a damn
'cuz her corneas are safe.
Prescription insoles.
Feelin' the flow.
Oldies playin' low
on her way to the sto'.
Pantyhose high.
Watch grandma fly.
27 in a 45.
Middle-fingers in her eye.
Grandma don't care.
She's cruising in her whip:
a tricked out, souped up
Honda Civic '96.
Sportin' 20-inch rims.
Can't barely see no rubber.
Got some flashing neon lights
on the bottom of that sucker.
Bright green paint job,
barely legal tints,
neon green wing

on the back of that thing.
Top speed 120,
but the engine's real loud.
She's drilled holes in the muffler
to make a deceptive sound.
When she drives by the high school,
all the homeboys go nuts:
"Even my pink Toyota
ain't that hooked up!"
She drives up to an intersection,
and stops at a light.
She looks out the window
to see some kid on a bike.
Grandma revs her engine,
stares this punk in the eye.
The kid stares back.
It's racing time.
The light turns green,
but Grandma's kinda slow.
The honking and cursing
can't make Grandma go.
In a short time, it's too late.
The kid is out of sight.
And Grandma's straight loungin'
at the same green light.
Grandma don't care.
She's chillin' in her whip,
Her souped up,
bright green Honda is the shit.

afterword

by alicia collura

When people ask if I have any siblings, I tell them I have an older brother. "Just the two of you?" "Yes, just the two of us." But, the truth is, I have two brothers. There is the brother I knew growing up — the one who gave me a stuffed alligator the day I was born, the one who hated when I tagged along with him and his older friends, the one who introduced me to David Lynch, Stanley Kubrick, Saves the Day, the one who, as we grew older, began turning to me for advice on girls and life. Then, there is the brother I am still getting to know — the one who lay in a coma for weeks, the one who I helped feed when he could not hold a spoon, the one who relearned to sit, type, speak, and walk, the one who inspires every person he meets with his resilience, determination, and wit. These brothers are, at once, the same person and two entirely different beings. This dichotomy — being of two minds, having lived in two bodies, understanding one truth while knowing others perceive a different reality — runs as a constant theme throughout this book.

If nothing else, I hope this book has left you, as it has me, pondering the duality of being and the gravity of perception. We all undergo metamorphoses in life. We grow up; we move on; we get old; we experience loss; we witness new life; we alter our views; we grow in our convictions. We do this standing on two legs or sitting on two wheels. Matt's story, which he shares with such acuteness and humor in these pages, exemplifies the reality that, in all our lives, inconsistency is the only constant. And, like Matt, by accepting inconsistency as an impetus rather than a deterrent, we can grow and learn. As my brother wrote so succinctly, "Things do not always stay constant. One thing that must stay constant is knowing how to adapt and doing the best with what you have."

UNCOMFORTABLE

READY

koobly/chorby/beebo/
choopy-style

FLUFFMAN, A LITTLE BABY